GERMANY

 **Marshall Cavendish**
Benchmark
New York

This edition first published in 2011 in
the United States of America by
Marshall Cavendish Benchmark.

Marshall Cavendish Benchmark
99 White Plains Road
Tarrytown, NY 10591
Website: www.marshallcavendish.us

© Marshall Cavendish International (Asia)
Pte Ltd 2011
Originated and designed by Marshall Cavendish
International (Asia) Pte Ltd
A member of Times Publishing Limited
Times Centre, 1 New Industrial Road
Singapore 536196

Written by: Richard Lord
Edited by: Crystal Chan
Designed by: Lock Hong Liang/Steven Tan
Picture research: Thomas Khoo

Library of Congress Cataloging-in-Publication Data
Lord, Richard.
Germany / by Richard Lord.
p. cm. -- (Festivals of the world)
Summary: "This book explores the exciting
culture and many festivals that are celebrated in
Germany"--Provided by publisher.
Includes index.
ISBN 978-1-60870-100-1
1. Festivals--Germany--Juvenile literature.
2. Germany--Social life and customs--
Juvenile literature. I. Title.
GT4850.A2L66 2011
394.26943--dc22
2009048271
ISBN 978-1-60870-100-1

Printed in Malaysia

1 3 6 5 4 2

Contents

It's Festival Time . . .

The German word for festival is *fest*. Germany is home to many exciting festivals, including one of the largest in the world—Oktoberfest. In addition, there is a carnival in Germany that can last for four or five months! Everybody dresses up in costumes, and there are plenty of good things to eat, such as sausages, pretzels, and delicious doughnuts. Come along and join the fun. It's festival time in Germany!

Where's Germany?

Germany is located in the middle of Europe. It has many neighbors and shares its border with nine other countries. A large area of the country is covered by mountains and forests, but in the north the land is flat. In 1949, Germany was divided into two countries—East Germany and West Germany. In 1990, the two countries became one again. Today, Germany is divided into sixteen states. The capital of the country is Berlin.

Who Are the Germans?

Many centuries ago, Germany was home to different tribes of people, including the Goths, Cimbri, and Vandals. In the fifth century, a tribe called the Franks invaded. Over time, the Franks forced the people to become Christian. Many centuries later, the Catholic Church and its leaders became very powerful and influential. Many believed the Catholic Church was taking advantage of the people. In 1517, a monk named Martin Luther protested against these abuses. He started a movement called the **Reformation**, which gave the people more religious freedom. Today people come to live in Germany from all over the world.

✳ This girl is wearing traditional German clothes.

GERMANY

* Neuschwanstein Castle in Bavaria may have served as a model for the Cinderella Castle in Walt Disney World's Magic Kingdom.

What Are the Festivals?

SPRING

* **Summer's Day**—Children wear brightly colored socks and march through the town to celebrate the end of winter.

* **Palm Sunday**—The Sunday before Easter when Christian children decorate palm branches with ribbons and eggshells.

* **Walpurgis Night**—Huge bonfires are lit during the Feast of the Witches to scare away bad spirits and to mark the arrival of spring.

* **May Day**—Villagers put up a pole used for May Day dances and games to celebrate spring.

* **Ascension Thursday**—A figure of Jesus Christ is drawn up to the top of the church to the sound of trumpets to represent Jesus's rise to heaven. This day is also Father's Day in Germany.

You can be sure of a devilishly good time on Walpurgis Night!

SUMMER

* **Feast of St. John the Baptist**—In remembrance of the saint, people push wheels to the top of a hill and set them on fire. These burning wheels are also ancient symbols that represent warmth and light.

* **Dinkelsbühler Kinderzeche**—Children and teachers have a feast to remember the day when children saved the town of Dinkelsbühl from Swedish troops who had come to invade.

* **Slaying of the Dragon**—A stage drama is acted out every year to bring to life the story of St. George and the Dragon.

AUTUMN

* **Oktoberfest**—This popular festival is best known for its food and drink. Today countries around the world have their own Oktoberfests!

* **Harvest Festival**—Villagers give thanks for the harvest and celebrate with a huge feast of fresh fruits, vegetables, and grains.

* **Cannstatter Volksfest**—The festival features singing, dancing, food, and drink. The main attraction is a giant wooden pillar decorated with fruit that is set up at the festival grounds.

* **All Saints' Day**—This feast day is held in honor of all the Christian saints.

* **St. Martin's Day**—A traditional holiday in remembrance of St. Martin, a Roman soldier who later became a bishop. Children mark the occasion by carrying paper lanterns, and families enjoy a roast goose dinner.

WINTER

* **St. Nikolaus Day**—Eager children put out their empty shoes in the hopes that St. Nikolaus will fill them up with gifts as a reward for good behavior.

* **Christmas**— An important Christian celebration to honor the birth of Jesus Christ.

* **St. Sylvester Day**—Young men wearing masks walk the streets making lots of noise to scare bad spirits away.

* **New Year's Day**—A holiday that falls on January 1, the first day of the year, according to the modern Gregorian calendar.

* **Feast of the Epiphany**—For this Christian holiday, children dress up as the three wise men and sing songs to people to wish them good luck.

* **Karneval**—A huge celebration with parades and masked balls, which is sometimes referred to as Germany's fifth season.

Come and join me for my very own festival—St. Nikolaus Day.

St. Martin's Day

Shortly after night falls on the evening of November 11, the streets of many cities and towns across Germany are filled with rows of lanterns. The lanterns light up the night sky. Soon a parade will begin. A man dressed up as a Roman soldier rides a horse at the front of the parade. This man plays the part of St. Martin. Children march behind the man on horseback holding tall, thin candles. Other children carry colorful paper lanterns.

✳ This sculpture shows St. Martin giving part of his cloak to the man in need.

Who Was St. Martin?

More than one thousand years ago, Martin was a soldier in the Roman army. It is believed that when he was returning from duty one cold night, he saw a freezing beggar. Martin was wearing a thick cloak to keep warm. Feeling pity for the beggar, Martin took out his sword, cut his heavy cloak in two, and gave half of it to the beggar. Martin went on to become a bishop in France. Today St. Martin is known as the **patron saint** of the poor.

Where Is Everyone Going?

After marching through the streets, all the people in the **procession** gather at a nearby church or school. There, someone reads the story of St. Martin and the beggar, and a play is performed on stage.

After the play is over, the children put their extra toys in a box. The toys are then given to others who are less fortunate.

Finally, a giant bonfire is lit. The bonfire blazes until it finally burns out. After that, everyone drinks a cup of hot cider and eats special St. Martin's Day cakes to keep warm.

✳ People used to believe that by dancing around a blazing bonfire they could keep the winter away. A saying in Germany goes: "Winter does not joke anymore after St. Martin's Day."

A Protestant Festival, Too

The German leader Martin Luther was born on November 10, 1483, almost the same day as St. Martin, but more than one thousand years later. Protestants like to remember Luther on St. Martin's Day, even though the day was not actually named for him.

✳ In the past, St. Martin's Day marked the beginning of winter, long nights, and the need to work by candlelight. This may be how the tradition of carrying candles and lanterns on St. Martin's Day began.

THINK ABOUT THIS

St. Martin gave up half his cloak to keep the beggar warm. Do you know any other stories about people who have helped others in need? Have you ever helped someone less fortunate?

* Some of the paper lanterns that people carry on St. Martin's Day are sold in shops, but most of them are made by the children at school. These children are holding lanterns they made that look like owls.

A St. Martin's Day Poem

Lantern, Lantern
Sun, moon, and stars
Burn up my light,
Burn up my light
But don't burn my
dear Lantern

On the night of the parade, parents help children light candles inside the lanterns.

Karneval

At the end of January or the beginning of February, very strange things start happening in Germany. People of all ages can be seen dressing up in bright costumes, painting their faces, and dancing in the streets! Restaurant and shop owners hang streamers and other colorful decorations all over the town. This is *Karneval* [CAR-nay-val], which is known as Germany's fifth season. In some parts of Germany, Karneval is called *Fastnacht* [FAHS-knockt] or *Fasching* [FAH-sching]. Whatever it is called, it is always a time for people to celebrate and have fun.

✳ These girls are enjoying the delicious foods that are available on the streets during Karneval—berliner and sausages.

The Start of Karneval

Officially, Karneval begins in November, but the events do not usually start until late January or February. At this time, the signs of the festival can be seen all over Germany. The beginning of Karneval is called *Tolle Tage* [TOLL-eh TAHG-eh], which means crazy days in German. On the last day of Karneval, there is a big parade with floats. Lots of people march in the parade, wearing bright costumes and masks. There are always bands in the parades, too, and people dance and sing in the streets. People eat special foods, especially **berliner** [bair-LEEN-er], plump jelly donuts that street stands sell during Karneval season.

✳ During Karneval's Fool's Congress, people are awarded prizes for the craziest costumes and the funniest speeches.

✳ The marching bands are an important part of Karneval festivities. They make music for people to dance to. As the procession reaches the main square, the crowds begin to yell for sweets. Then thousands of chocolate bars and candies are thrown into the streets for people to collect.

Women's Day

The Thursday before **Lent** during Karneval season is called Women's Day. This day is reserved for women to dress in costumes and to do mischievous things. In some cities, women storm City Hall and take the key to the city from the mayor. Once they have the key, women are allowed to do whatever they please for the rest of the day.

How Did Karneval Begin?

When the Karneval celebration first started hundreds of years ago, it was for a very special reason. After almost three months of cold, dark weather, people had grown tired of the winter. To try to make spring come back earlier, the people dressed up in masks and costumes and made a lot of noise. They believed that if they were scary enough, they might scare winter away.

* Germans have a saying that "whoever is not foolish at Karneval is foolish for the rest of the year." Anyone who disapproves of the celebration is called *Karnevalsmuffel* [CAR-nay-val SMOO-full], or a carnival grouch.

The Last Hurrah

Later, Karneval was a time for people to have fun before Lent. Lent is the period of fasting before Easter when Christians think about the suffering of Jesus Christ. All festivals were canceled during Lent, so Karneval was the last time before Easter that people could really celebrate.

THINK ABOUT THIS

On what day of the year do many Americans dress up in costumes and masks? How is this holiday different from the German Karneval festival?

Did You Know?

The English word *carnival* has the same meaning as the German word *karneval*. Both words come from another language called Latin. In Latin, "*Carne, vale!*" means goodbye, meat. This is because Christians are supposed to give up meat during the forty days of Lent. Karneval time was their last chance to enjoy meat.

* During Karneval, policemen line the streets to keep the procession in order. Even though their job is serious, sometimes they join in the fun.

St. Nikolaus Day and Christmas

Think about living in a country where Santa Claus comes more than once a year! For Christian children in Germany, both Santa Claus and Saint Nikolaus are part of Christmastime celebrations.

St. Nikolaus Day

On the night of December 5, German children put their shoes outside their doors before they go to bed. They do this in hope that St. Nikolaus will come. Typically, in the morning, their shoes are either filled with candies, cookies, and other small gifts, or nothing but a stick.

Who Was St. Nikolaus?

St. Nikolaus was a **bishop** in the Catholic Church. He was famous for his kindness to children. According to one story, he left three pieces of gold on a windowsill for three poor girls one night. The gold rolled off the windowsill and landed in stockings that had been hung by the fire to dry. This is where the tradition of hanging stockings by the chimney comes from.

✳ Sometimes the figure of St. Nikolaus makes children recite a prayer or a poem before giving them a present.

Naughty and Nice

It is thought that when St. Nikolaus comes to visit, he brings along a book in which all the names of bad children are written. His helper, Knecht Ruprecht, carries a sack filled with presents and a birch rod or stick. The rod is for all the children who have misbehaved that year. The presents are for all the children who have been good.

What Does St. Nikolaus Look Like?

The legendary figure of Santa Claus is based on St. Nikolaus. Both figures wear a big white beard and a red-and-white costume. In fact, St. Nikolaus's costume is very similar to the one bishops used to wear many years ago.

* Children's choirs are popular during the Christmas season. The choir sings songs dedicated to St. Nikolaus.

This display is part of the famous Christmas market in Nuremberg. It begins on the Friday before the first Sunday in Advent.

Christmas

In Germany, the Christmas season begins about four weeks before Christmas Day, when *Weihnachtsmärkte* [VY-knocks-MAIRK-ta], or Christmas markets, start opening. These are huge, outdoor markets filled with stands. Each stand sells something different—decorations, gifts, and good things to eat and drink.

Christmas Eve, December 24, is the most important day in the Christmas season. This is the day when families get together to sing Christmas carols, open gifts, and eat a big dinner, usually roast goose and red cabbage. It is also the day when most German families decorate their Christmas trees.

Advent means coming in Latin. For one month before Christmas, Christians celebrate the coming of Jesus Christ.

THINK ABOUT THIS

Do you know the poem about old St. Nick? Does your family celebrate at Christmastime?

Advent

During the Christmas season, German Christians hang **Advent** wreaths in their homes. Every Sunday for four weeks before Christmas, someone in the family lights a candle and puts it in the wreath. By Christmas day, four candles are lit. An even more welcome sign of the beginning of the Christmas season is the Advent calendar. These special calendars begin December 1 and run only up to December 24. The best thing about the calendar is that behind each date is a small door. When opened, each door reveals a gift, usually candies or cakes. The two best gifts are almost always behind the doors for December 6 (St. Nikolaus Day) and December 24 (Christmas Eve).

In late December, the Sun starts moving back toward Earth for the first time in six months. The early tribes of Germany celebrated the return of the Sun by decorating trees with candles.

Christmas Trees

Many people think the tradition of decorating trees at Christmastime started in Germany. According to one story, Martin Luther was walking home from church one night. The countryside was so beautiful he wanted to share it with his family. He dug up a small fir tree, brought it into the house, and decorated it with colorful stars and tiny candles.

Oktoberfest

In autumn, many towns and villages in Germany have special harvest festivals. These festivals are a way for farmers to celebrate a good harvest. Local festivals usually have lots of food, especially harvest foods, like fruits, vegetables, and grains.

✳ On the first Sunday of Oktoberfest there is a huge parade with horse-drawn carts, floats, and people wearing traditional German clothing, like this young woman. The procession starts at the Bavarian State Parliament and travels through the town to the fairground.

The Biggest Festival

The biggest and most famous of Germany's many harvest festivals is Munich's Oktoberfest. It became large because Munich is one of Germany's most popular cities. Thousands of people come from all over Germany and from all over the world to visit Oktoberfest.

When Is Oktoberfest?

Many people think that Oktoberfest starts in October, but don't be fooled. In fact, it starts in late September and runs for sixteen days through early October.

Let the Party Begin

Before the celebration begins, the city organizes a parade through the streets of Munich. The parade ends at a fairground, called the *Theresienwiese* [tear-RAY-zee-en-VEE-za], or Therese's Meadow. The fairground is a huge, open meadow, but during Oktoberfest it is covered with tents that can hold thousands of people.

A big carnival is set up around the tents. Musicians walk through the fairground playing traditional Bavarian music. Munich is located in the state of Bavaria. Many Bavarian traditions come alive during Oktoberfest.

✳ The entrance to the fairgrounds is surrounded by carnival rides. There is a roller coaster in the shape of a figure eight, a shooting range, giant swings, not to mention attractions like a hall of mirrors.

Origins of Oktoberfest

One of the things that makes Oktoberfest so special is the way it began. In 1810, the Crown Prince of Bavaria married Princess Therese von Sachsen-Hildburghausen. The prince was so happy about his marriage that he invited everyone in the kingdom to his wedding party. More than 40,000 people attended the event. The wedding celebration was such a success that the people of Munich decided to do it again every year. The fairground where Oktoberfest takes place is named after Princess Therese.

❋ Each year at Oktoberfest, a huge mechanical lion is set up outside the Löwenbräu tent. The lion is the national symbol of Bavaria, and the symbol for Löwenbräu, one of Germany's biggest breweries.

❋ The name *pretzel* actually comes from the Latin word for arm, *brachium*. The German word for pretzel is *brezel*. German pretzels are delicious, easy to hold, and fun to eat.

Glorious Food

Since Oktoberfest is one of Germany's great harvest festivals, one of the highlights is the food. There are stands of every shape and size at Oktoberfest selling all kinds of special German foods. What are German foods? Pretzels, sauerkraut, and dumplings, just to name a few. However, the favorite fare at Oktoberfest is barbecued chicken, white sausage, and oxen.

✳ Hats with feathers like this one can be seen all over Bavaria during Oktoberfest. They are called *gamsbart* [GEMS-bart] and are part of traditional Bavarian dress. *Lederhosen* [lead-air-HOH-zen] are leather shorts often worn with suspenders. Green woolen jackets, coats, and shorts make up the rest of the outfit.

Walpurgis Night

Suddenly, the dark sky is lit up with the blaze of torches and bonfires. People dressed as witches carry broomsticks and pitchforks. They start dancing around bonfires. Finally, a person dressed as the devil arrives and gives a speech. Walpurgis Night is a time when Germans dress up in frightening costumes to celebrate the Feast of the Witch.

* Witch hunts began in the fifteenth century. At that time, some people believed stories that witches flew to the Brocken and bit off pieces of church bells along the way to bring to the devil.

* In the past, on Walpurgis Night, people put on scary masks to frighten away people they thought might be spying on them. Those people who knew the witches' password were invited to join the feast.

Witch Hunt

The festival is held on the night of April 30 in Germany's Harz Mountains. People sing and dance around the bonfires in their costumes and scary masks. The highlight of the night´s festivities comes just before midnight, when a dummy dressed to look like a witch is burned in the fire as a **sacrifice** to the devil. When midnight strikes, a person playing the May Queen suddenly appears. She is the symbol of everything that is good. She chases away the devils and witches until next year's festival.

The Brocken

An old German story says that witches held their annual **coven**, or witches' group, on the Brocken, the highest peak in the Harz Mountains. The Brocken is also said to be where the devil came to meet the witches. When East and West Germany were divided, and the West Germans could not go to the Brocken anymore, they started celebrating Walpurgis Night in other places. Today, there are at least five towns in the Harz Mountains that celebrate Walpurgis Night festivals.

✳ These women are dressed as witches in celebration of Walpurgis Night.

THINK ABOUT THIS

The original Walpurgis Night festival was a time to celebrate the coming of spring. A dummy was thrown into the fire to burn away the last traces of winter. Then the May Queen arrived, a springtime symbol.

Things for You to Do

The four Sundays leading up to Christmas are called Advent. Advent is an important time in Germany. People celebrate Advent in many different ways. Some people light one candle each Sunday before Christmas. One popular activity for German children is to make an Advent calendar.

What is an Advent Calendar?

An Advent calendar is usually a picture with twenty-four numbered windows cut into it, one for each of the days before Christmas. Behind each window is a little surprise. On some calendars, the surprise may be a picture. On others, it might be a piece of candy or a little toy. Starting with December 1, a window is opened each day until Christmas.

Here's how to make a simple Advent calendar. Be as creative as possible when putting together the calendar.

Make an Advent Calendar

Draw a Christmas picture on a rectangular piece of cardboard using markers or colored pencils. Copy one of ours or make your own. Arrange twenty-four squares around your picture and number them one through twenty-four. Cut three sides of each square to make a window. Put the picture over a piece of paper and trace the squares onto the paper. Cut out pictures from an old magazine and glue them in the squares on the paper, or write messages to yourself about the number of days until Christmas. When you've finished with all twenty-four squares, line up the squares behind the windows and glue the paper to the cardboard.

FURTHER INFORMATION

Books: *A to Z: Germany.* Jeff Reynolds (Children's Press, 2005).

Festive Foods! Germany. Sylvia Goulding (Chelsea Clubhouse, 2008).

The Legend of St. Nicholas: A Story of Christmas Giving. Dandi Daley Mackall (Zonderkidz, 2007).

The Secret World of Hildegard. Jonah Winter (Arthur A. Levine Books, 2007).

Websites: germanoriginality.com/heritage/tradition.php—Offers easy-to-read information on a variety of well-known German holiday traditions.

http://kids.britannica.com/comptons/article-9274536/Germany—This website provides interesting and detailed facts about Germany and its history.

Make a St. Martin's Day Lantern

Make your own lantern like the ones children carry through the streets on the evening of St. Martin's Day. You can choose whatever design you like. When you are finished, hang the lantern up in your room.

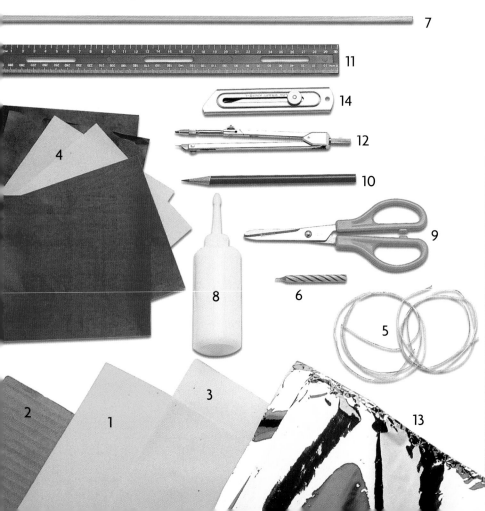

You will need:

1. Two strips of heavy construction paper; 1 by 19 inches (2.5 cm by 48 cm) and 2 by 19 inches (5 cm by 48 cm)
2. Cardboard
3. A piece of sturdy transparent paper 19 by 10 inches (48 cm by 25 cm)
4. Colored tissue paper
5. Two pieces of wire 12–13 inches (30–33 cm) long
6. A large birthday candle
7. A 20-inch (50-cm) dowel
8. Glue
9. Scissors
10. Pencil
11. Ruler
12. Compass
13. Gold paper, cut in strips, 2 by 19 inches (5 cm by 48 cm) and 3/4 by 19 inches (2 cm by 48 cm)
14. Craft knife to be used by an adult helper

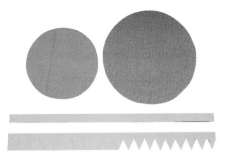

1 Cut two circles from the cardboard, one 6 inches (15 cm) across, the other 6 1/2 inches (16.5 cm). Draw a line across the wider construction paper strip 1 1/4 inches (3.2 cm) from the bottom. Cut teeth up to this line.

2 Bend the teeth under and glue them along the edge of the bigger circle. Glue the ends of the strip together.

3 Make a slit in the middle of the small circle. Wind the wire around the candle and attach it to the cardboard. Glue the small circle to the bigger circle.

4 Cut out designs from the colored paper and glue them to the transparent paper. Glue the 1 inch- (2.5 cm-) strip to the inside of the lantern at the top. Glue the narrow gold paper strip to the bottom. Cut a fringe in the other strip and glue it to the top. Glue the lantern body to the turned-up edge of the cardboard. Glue the ends together.

5 Hook the ends of the wire through the top of the lantern. Twist the middle of the wire into a loop and slide the stick through the loop. Have an adult light the candle.

29

Make Kinderglüwein

*K*inderglüwein [KIN-der-GLUE-vine] is a very popular cold weather drink in Germany. It can be found at all the festivals in November and December. This cider is often prepared at home during the Christmas season. It may be served with German Christmas cookies, cakes, and grilled sausages. It not only tastes good, it is healthy, too.

You will need:

1. 1 quart (1 liter) grape juice, cherry juice, or apple juice
2. 4 whole cloves
3. 2 cinnamon sticks
4. 1 tablespoon lemon juice
5. A pinch of cardamom
6. Half an apple, thinly sliced, with an adult's help
7. Measuring spoons
8. A saucepan
9. A knife, to be used by an adult helper
10. A wooden spoon
11. A ladle
12. A cutting board

1 Pour the juice into the saucepan.

2 Add the spices and lemon juice.

3 Have an adult help you turn on the burner under the pan. Put in the apple slices and turn down the heat.

5 Take the saucepan off the stove and pour the drink into cups using a ladle. Drink while it is still warm. *Prost!*— that's German for "Cheers!"

4 Let the drink simmer at a low heat for 5–10 minutes. The longer it cooks, the stronger the flavor.

Glossary

Advent	A time for Christians to celebrate the coming of the Christmas season.
berliner	Jelly-filled doughnuts, especially popular during Karneval.
bishop	A leader in the Catholic Church.
coven	A group of witches.
Karnevalsmuffel	Someone who does not participate in the fun during Karneval.
lederhosen	Traditional Bavarian leather shorts often worn with suspenders.
Lent	The forty days before Easter when Christians think about the suffering of Jesus Christ.
patron saint	A saint whose protection is dedicated to a certain place or group of people.
procession	A trip to a holy place, or a parade of people.
Reformation	The reform of the Catholic Church started by Martin Luther.
sacrifice	Destroying something in a religious ceremony.

Index

Photo Credits
Alamy/Photolibrary: 3 (top), 4, 5, 8, 17, 22 (top), 24 (bottom); Bavaria Bildagentur: 9 (top), 10, 11 (bottom), 18; Bildarchiv Huber: 11 (top), 29; David Simson: cover, 1, 2 (bottom), 12; Deustche Zentrale für Tourismus: 3 (bottom), 6 (bottom), 13 (bottom), 14 (bottom), 20, 21 (bottom), 22 (bottom), 23, 25; Fremdenverkhrsamt: 6 (top), 24 (top); Getty Images: 7 (top), 19 (top); Inter Nationes: 9 (bottom),14 (top), 15; Photolibrary: 7 (bottom), 16; The Image Bank: 21 (top); Travel Ink: 13 (top), 19 (bottom)

19.95